Of Meadows and Echoes:

The Yearning for Soft Spaces

Of Meadows and Echoes:

The Yearning for Soft Spaces by

Khalil Elayan

© 2025 Khalil Elayan. All rights reserved.
This material may not be reproduced in any form, published,
reprinted, recorded, performed, broadcast,
rewritten or redistributed without
the explicit permission of Khalil Elayan.
All such actions are strictly prohibited by law.

Cover design by Shay Culligan
Cover image by Anna Davis
Author photo by Anna Davis

ISBN: 978-1-63980-805-2
Library of Congress Control Number: 2025947191

Kelsay Books
502 South 1040 East, A-119
American Fork, Utah 84003
Kelsaybooks.com

For Anna, who painted my first meadow . . .

Acknowledgments

Thank you to the following publications, in which versions of these poems previously appeared:

The Black Fork Review: "The Pelican Walk"
The Esthetic Apostle: "The Fissure People"
Plants & Poetry Journal: "Alma Verde," "Of Meadows and Echoes," "Wild Duck Persuasion"
Poet's Choice: "The Horizon of Knowing," "Noontime Caress," "The Last Sky"
Snapdragon: A Journal of Art & Healing: "St. Moling's Well," "Descent of the Night Purple"
Talking Writing: "Seasonal"
The Trumpeter: "Sunset Fray"
Wild Roof Journal: "Stay"
Wingless Dreamer: "At the Altar of the Blackberry Bush," "Popular Poplar," "The Swarm"
The Write Launch: "Of Voices, Waters, and Fires," "Rock Paper Pictures," "Samsara Serenade"

Special thanks to: Christopher Ghattas, David Marsh, Shara Smith, and my parents.

Contents

Part I. Aborning

Alma Verde	15
Of Meadows and Echoes	18
St. Moling's Well	20
Wild Duck Persuasion	23
The Lost Zephyr	25
The Horizon of Knowing	26
Noontime Caress	27
Eos	28

Part II. Burgeoning

Sunset Fray	33
Of Voices, Waters, and Fires	34
Rosehips at the Gates of Dawn	36
At the Altar of the Blackberry Bush	38
A Dancer Among Dandelions	40
Siddhartha Song	42

Part III. Tendering

Stay	45
Rock Paper Pictures	49
The Fissure People	52
Mountain Pass Blues	54
The Pelican Walk	56
and the clouds were whales	59

Part IV. Reaping

Seasonal	65
Popular Poplar	67
The Descent of the Night Purple	68
The Swarm	70
The Last Sky	72
The Lost Quiet	75
Samsara Serenade	77

Part I. Aborning

Alma Verde

have you forgotten the touch
of a wet leaf on the ball of your foot,
the feeling of sap, dew, and decay
as you peel it off

or to twist your finger 'round
a vine that curls a fence top
and tip your tongue in its
honeysuckle nectar

when did you last lay
on a carpet of pine needles
and caress the underside of
a mushroom and catalogue

its gills with your thumbnail . . .

the eye of the forest
opens wide to all who
are foreign to its secret
sounds

yet when was the last time
you heard the cry
of an animal unknown,
alone in the dark

the mystery as clear,
now, as the ache in an
old foot, too worn out
to walk an unbeaten path

will you peer from a great stump
at an out-of-warren litter of hares
circle-hopping an alpha,
content in his mouth twisting

and watch the euphoria of young
hind legs spring load into the ether.
this is the taste of a secluded hollow
in yonder days of virgin green

all woods have heartbeats,
each to their own rhythms
and spirits that never die but
do cry in anguish

at crimes in their midst,
big and small.

a salutation would be nice,
palm, upended in reverence,
a breath, taken deep behind
your heart

and then a half turn of the hand,
a mild caress of the atmosphere
that congregation of old oaks has given
you

then to find a rugged branch
in a dry leaf pile by an edge,
long eroded by weeping winds
at dusk

take it as your staff and
make a way heard in the forest
and echoed in your future
so that you know

where it was you conducted
your *thump thump pat* against
wet bark and dry clumps

the nook and cranny of a
wrinkled brow can tell a story,
too, as you look through leaf
upon leaf

at the white star jutting
a ray into your path

recalling the ballad of your affair
with quiet queries to the
shadow that encircled you
in the breast of all that is holy

Of Meadows and Echoes

There is a soft space
        of wildflowers and seeding grasses

Where the rabbits chew clover buds
        and nestle in curling blades of emerald

At dawn, a mourning dove's serenade
        cooing from the cherry blossoms

There is a wide space
        of dandelions and mouse whiskers

Where gaps in the bulrushes
        allow climbing turtles to lay their eggs

And the noontime dragonfly
        swizzles on stalk or stem

There is a shady place
        at the root of a red oak

Where nuts and gatherers meet
        to sprawl in shadowed quiet

At dusk, the robin calls and calls
        and the worm burrows fast

There is a soft space
        down in the rolling meadow of echoes

St. Moling's Well

Back at the café, Mark says
in an east Irish accent that
it was the prettiest little spot in all
the world

So I make my way out
between the stone of the place
and the River Barrow
where the salmon are jumping

A narrow valley Riverwalk
where rain and sleet and sun
all come down and out
in the matter of minutes

It's up the hill I go
toward nesting rooks in naked trees
near the old cemetery
in the yard of the ruined abbey

It is here I can look
        down
at the spot where pilgrims stood
after many miles unswerving

A place that bloomed
with beatitudes
acute sensibility
and ancient peace

A man, dirtied by carpenter's dust
bars the path to the well
A suspicious look—tossed over his shoulder
falls at my feet

Another day, I say
to the stone wall,
border to the path of the watering hole
the monk had blessed

Perhaps the rude looking man
will turn to stone
as those who toiled on Patron Day . . .
who did not honor the circle of pilgrims

But a good look I did get
of that little spot where the stream pooled;
where it met a holy man
who gave it a legend

There, a cure lay for those who
would dip a tired foot,
and those who'd encircle
and recite

Hail Marys and Our Fathers
are recorded in the roots of
dead trees—
and the cracks of stone walls

Perhaps each rock is a prayer
caught fast in the trail to heaven,
a place where weary travelers
escape death

And where all I wanted
was to kiss a ripple
upon the prettiest little spot
in all the world

Wild Duck Persuasion

The pond in March
brings strange swimmers

Small, wiggling, teardrop
tadpoles pirouette young algae

Pear petals and Maple buds
float on surface rings
made by soft zephyrs

Long grass tips bend
backwards and forwards
to intersect needles of pine in
surface play

A muskrat may bisect
the pond in transmigration
from north den to south den

Bits of hickory bark float
like alligator scales, and
circle round and round
before soaking in the deep

But it is the goose in her soft
brown, black, and beige down
that sees an outlier

A wild duck, alone in his
reverie, smaller than her
grand anxiety at being harried
by prospective lovers

She does not know a moment of peace,
charged by two males,
lustful in their Canadian flight

They goad her in mock takeoffs
slapping wingtips on waking water,
as treetops hover like arena watchers

The duck wants no involvement
Preferring access to the pond
in quasi-absentia

His is a philosophy of quiescence,
a passive swimmer among titans
of sword and seed

Again, the goose marvels at his
majestic mildness, his tonic
of purpose

As she scoots to center and edge
and bank, in hopes that his repose
can be hers

The Lost Zephyr

Where are the breezes that carried me
        across streets and fields and valleys
like soft balloons filled with universal gasses?

Cradled by nature's breath, I was raised
        like a goblet, toasting the firmament
where the gods reside and plunder our kinetic drives.

Is it the way to forget that blowing muses were
        once so prevalent on Wednesdays
at noon in the March month or the April sun?

I taste the spirit mint on the edges of gales and gusts;
        it is still there, that fossil sense of remembering
when a ghost wind sallied to our side.

Oh, invisible magic carpet that floated me to
        infinite horizons, give me the antidote
to this staticity of form and future!

Dare my body to utter its undulation
        in modes unknown to silent words,
and feed me the nectar of wincing eyes.

I am taken by the hand of a fleeting cloud
to a chilly hollow of echoes.

The Horizon of Knowing

I have made a discovery
that has close-pinned my soul

And though a color *can* make a sound,
is it not better to sing a picture of your love
as you smell the grass seed beneath your nails

when standing with wet feet in soft nettles?

To cough a hue into the ether—
To hear the echo in a heartbeat of memory—
To forsake all fossilized fear—

This is what it means to give way
to an atmosphere

and awaken in the horizon of knowing

exactly what it means to pass beyond the stale story
of weariness

To drink the ambrosia of peace atop
snow driven peaks of nameless nations.

Noontime Caress

It is not a specific view or place,
nor a tree or brook,
not even a type of toad or thrush,
just a feeling, really—a texture
gone wrong . . .

The very atmosphere, as
it caresses my arm in
summer—at noon
when the sun's rays
pummel my crown

It is then that I know
the sky has fallen
heavily on my skin
and the world is
terribly different . . .

Eos

Homer spoke of dawns,
rosy-fingered, yawning mornings
of delight and play

My dawns yearn
for the sun of all suns

A morning star, pooling
the horizon with pumpkin
and tangerine

I can taste her in
infinite universes, being born
to a million trillion skies

A pulsating bloom of endless energy

I want to touch her, to
steal her away from the blue
expanse

And bring her to my table,
like a mimosa in a teacup

To drink her down

There, somewhere in my
in-between

She will light a fire in my ribs

And my short, quick breaths
will feed her flames

She burns inside me
       . . . exquisitely
My mouth opens as a cave
that drinks a ray
from the sunrise star

Part II. Burgeoning

Sunset Fray

When beaded algae like floating Styrofoam pebbles cover the pond, I know May is here. Nestled near a blue wood, perhaps or perhaps not fed by an underground spring and with low hanging marsh oaks and willows weeping into the pond's surface, empurpled bluegill males target all that come near nesting females and their eggs with the ferocity of great whites biting into seal butter. Bigmouths are known to interfere, to shoot like angry newspapers from teenage hands into the fray of underwater nest and egg and essence . . .

Unseen phalluses mean little in the midst of pointed fins and purposed mouths, and this is what I know best, this world of ripple and strike, of amber and green, of purpled empowerment, and of soft sunset on the surface of all that is holy to me. I take it with me, having been burned into my retinas, and it becomes a silent swing in my brain, lulling me to dream of what I did just hours before. As I amble the steps to the door, I regret not taking a little more time to see who would win the match between bass and bream. Bream pointing outwards from the nest's sphere like musk oxen in deep snow and the bass like wolves with big mouths yawning to eat the calf in the center of all that must go on . . .

Of Voices, Waters, and Fires

There it is—the horn of awakening. I submit to its call the way ancient tribes adored the mountains of the moon and the way fireflies soar over soft summer grasses escaping from the hot earth—caught in mid atmosphere between the ether and the soil . . . in perfect pitch and light. My affirmation becomes the resistant verdure of ancient trees of the North and of the scarlet wildflower that blooms from the crack of a rock so old it forgot it was rock and thought it was fertile earth so young. Then, giving birth to crimson explosion, it morphs into a rainbow of mesas jutting into the horizon of western skies, allotting valleys and nooks their respective triumphs as they meander their way through haunted passages. This becomes the floodwater plain of my adoration, eroding all walls, permeating all barriers, eviscerating all fear. In this flow, perpetual present is infinitely directed and time is linear no more. A voice—part of an old language, with a kind of sweetness that feeds the Redwoods and Sequoias of ancient births and seeps into spirit waters from ethereal sources in misty glens—this voice—becomes a channel that demystifies the world, irreversible in its foundational tenets of authenticity. I am shaken the way the wind cracks the shell of an acorn before it hits the earth, as to get the green snail out of hiding from the orb of plant and seed, to spring from each encounter into the oak of promise. In the darkness, there is the smoke of old fires. I can no longer smell what started them. The torrents of spring will soon extinguish the vestiges of the smoky remains and—tomorrow, the world will be winked at by the sun, nudging the arch in the foot of time that circles back onto itself, reminding me of the long grass that bends back to kiss the earth. Now, the rest of my life can tumble like happy children down a grassy hill

at summer's end

Rosehips at the Gates of Dawn

There was a time I tasted you
When I savored your birth and bloom
And like a wave of forgotten sun
You came crashing into me

There was a time I tasted you
Upon Bosnian flatbread
Bought from the dry, smooth hands
Of Ahmed, the grocer

There was a time I tasted you
Spread thick and thin
Upon the knife of reckoning
You made a tart out of my tongue

There was a time I tasted you
When you flooded my sensibilities
And gave verisimilitude to my
Every waking want

There was a time I tasted you
In the nights of coffee hangovers
Spliced with Irish and St-Germain
Making Americanos Bohemians

There was a time I tasted you
Your blood rose on the hip
Of the ocean's shore
Growing in bushy splendor

There was a time I tasted you
When I was at the gates of dawn

At the Altar of the Blackberry Bush

There is a great divining truth to blackberry picking.
And not yet dark,
the white moon of absolution shines forth,

giving testament to little things:
that bit of red pulp in purple cluster,
the brown spider wolfing its way through

blade and stalk, or the June bug
with rump against rump,
nestled in leafy crevasse.

These are nature's musings
in the twilight of reaching
round a jawline of thorns

to harvest the fruit of Phoenician hue,
while the twitter of swallow and seesaw sound
of mourning dove

serenade my pluck and prick.
And what crimson fluid baptizes
the storied leaves upon this swaying

stalk? The bowed and fruited bush
that thirsts for sacrificial bleeding.
It is the heyday of bursting baskets

and scratched skin, just there
beneath the nail, guarded by a bit
of armor too small to stay the

cordial of my efforts that cascades
down to the yellowed turf and the
den of beetle, an annual bloodletting

required before cobbler or jam
can set table. As I suck the source,
the blackberry awaits its desserts.

A Dancer Among Dandelions

An artist's palette lies on a side
in the midst of petal and stem,

colors splotched and dripping
from wood to earth and grasses.

But it is the arch of her foot
that hugs the base of a dandelion,

the purposed toes, dancing
in yellows and greens.

An artist's hair may billow in the wind
yet her feet skip fields of flowers.

Most at home with brush in hand
and naked in the verdure of spring,

she paints pictures of dapper lions
in the bush, and of dancing damsels

on the plain. Stained fingertips
scratch her chin and push wisps aside,

twirling the imaginary dress
she left on the hard, dry floor

preferring paint and earth and
grass and seed.

Her skin ripples in the sun,
freckled by the attention the

universe has given her.

Siddhartha Song

the hand
a pillar of clay
stoically stoned in midair
but salutation nonetheless
there is a season
for giving and severing
a fish
and some bread
a bit of blood
on a block of wood
the carpenter sucks his thumb
and builds a Walden
a celebration of sound
and silence
this is the way
and the not
to the fair
and to the picnic
he dares not go
a kite flies
a glint in the eye
of spectral oddity

Part III. Tendering

Stay

There's a place in a dream
—there, where the green river
infiltrates a wooded cove,

where a tired spirit
hides in the bark of a dead tree
and whispers to cracked leaves.

But where does the spirit go
when the bark breaks,
when the tree falls

and rude elbows are formed
where there was long, unbroken
purpose—a place to snuggle and spy

a wren lighting on a thicket
or the possum in its den. Perhaps a
drop in the still pool of the river's edge

betrays a squirrel's lost meal. These
are the reflections of a displaced memory
looking for a new nook to own.

The memory has abandoned the mind
that first remembered it. It's a runaway,
loosed in the land of the green river.

But this is my dream, my secret garden.
Why is it here wrestling with its destiny?
I know its source.

I know where it comes from.
But in the instant of recognition,
I lose the tangible moment

that could define its loss, that
could take it to its ambivalent host.
The home of nestling creatures

beckons to all, but this is a place
that does not recognize fear
or the zones of departed memories.

How do I make green rivers and dry dens
understand the plight of this poor spirit?
And tell it to come in from the cold

and set by the soft bank on a mild
afternoon. To rest its quivering
invisibility like an unwanted wraith.

"I know where you come from,"
I say aloud. "I know your source . . .
You have forsaken the forgetful one,

the one imprisoned by the purgatory
of fear." The memory recoils at my
familiarity, not wanting to understand

how it got here. We have both sought
refuge in the same place. I do not want it
to leave. "STAY," I cry aloud.

"I know you . . . I, too, was there,
as you were forming in the activity
of the source. I loved the one

who bore you on the shoulders
of forgetfulness. Yours is a destiny
of pilgrims without purpose."

But the spirit is gone, heedless
to my entreaties. It has found
a petrified forest in which to roam.

It cannot nestle in a piece of bark or
in a possum's den, and in no glen to
quiver, it bounces from rock to rock

shaking in its fitful mania. Now alone,
I drink from green waters and offer a
hand from which the wren will perch

and sing a song of delightful reverie.
I bury my feet in the thrift of the bank
and wink at a branch that touches the sun.

Rock Paper Pictures

It's called The Cave of Forgotten Dreams
this place where handprints
with broken finger
wave at squint-eyed scientists

where prehistoric rhino, too,
looks up and down
in animated
horn thrusting

It is a place
where I can no longer walk
       freely

into

its mouth,
for me to trace
the jowls of a saber tooth

or

to feel at home
in the chilled darkness

that once belonged to
a long dead tribe
of southern France

that hunted
and hooped
and hollered

their way from hunter gatherer
to farmer

Though I have yet to cross
its threshold
the history of the place

humps its way to caress
my innermost cheekbones
with an icy forefinger

and mesmerize me with
fireside chats about
arrow and bone and hide
of meat and fire
on picture and pride

These are ancient ones
who delved into
stone-walled comic books

the hero of which
was hunted and killed
ingested and digested

and immortalized on rock paper

The Fissure People

A fissure in the gorge
was the last thing I expected but
as the water issued forth

in a whirlpool of decadent clarity
I felt the suffering of centuries in a place
called the tear duct of infinite sorrow
by a tribe that predated the Cherokee.

Tadpoles the color of kidneys
underwater skipped away from my
wading legs that knew not their

trajectory in swirling waters that
superseded my own force. This is where
nature rewrites my history, where it
erodes as it evolves.

Geology says the Appalachians are
older than the Rockies and I quiver at the path
an ancient arrow arched its way towards

deer or elk. It is written in stone
how old the dead may be and how little
the living remember of ancient cracks in
their genealogy.

The arrow finds its home in the base of my memory tacking a hieroglyph from regretful spirits in the spectrum of a sleepwalker coming to drink from the source.

Mountain Pass Blues

A mountain pass is neither a road nor a well-worn path.
It's a narrow, ragged trail, much of which
is found by accident.
One may use the trunks of young trees as levers or handles, to push
upon as one rises.
Rocks, recently given birth to by wind and rain,
scattering old pieces of earth in the valley below,
these are the steppingstones to a higher ground,
atop which,
very few people look up. Most,
in their pride, look down at the place
left behind. Or, whether eager or worn out, at
the place they will go.
A curious traveler may feel encroached upon
by the denseness of the mountain wood or
the jagged hillside intruding upon the trail.
At the halfway point, the cresting traveler hears music,
a symphonic cacophony of eagle and owl,
wind cracking rock and limb. A strong gale
finds hollow and crevasse playing a haunting tune,
as a monk plays beneath Fuji's cherry,
blowing into an old flute, effortless the tortuous sound of lost love.
His monasticism as new as the traveler's synesthesia, stark,
hypnotic at the juncture where air is thin.

It is then that the one who walks the path
faces the echoes of duality, the place
where one self speaks and
the other flitters in the canyon below.
Is this the destiny of all mountain travelers?
To seek the source of sounds and selves?

To walk down the other side of the mountain
is to know what hides behind its face.
To travel a way spattered and sputtered by
rock and dirt and bone. The long way down
and down and down into shadow and secret.
This is the road to nonbeing, a time and place
of infinite possibility. Here, one can suck the sap
of an ancient maple and get just enough
energy to face the next hilltop rising into the sun.

The Pelican Walk

A quiet beach on one end,
a busy road on the other,
the elevated walk
        in-between.

This is how we make
our way back,
my daughter and I.

It is well-made . . .
It has to be!
To face the storm of wave
and swell.

To stand firm in flooded swirls.

Or to bake in August afternoons
when it gets hotter as it gets later.

Toes and sand and sandals
make thud, crunch, pop
on the firm wood,

the sounds of our shuffle.

Dusty shells clink in beach bags
and small pales echo, now empty
of towers after castle-making.

We are not alone on the walk.

Lizards, some green,
some sand-colored and
red-throated, hop with
incredible bursts, saluting
us with turning heads and
inquisitive,

rotating eyes.

We pass; they retreat.
And we look back and see
them descend into shadow.

The sky is birdless
but beautiful, melting
like tangerine sherbet
on a boy's T-shirt.

The beach, no longer visible,
I look to left and right at
scarlet flowers with yellow
edges, jutting into
       summer scorches.

Then without knowing it,
canopies arc, like folded
hands

and the walk becomes a place
of marsh and palmetto,
moss and magnolia,

bordered by infinite spectrum
of green.

I love this bit of path,

And so does the child next to me.

It's as if her breath, exhaled
into the ether is bartered for
by every branch, leaf, and petal

promising a perch to call her own.

But we are close to the end
with no pelican overhead.

I *must* see them, at least
one two or three, targeting
some flapping fish, a half
mile away,

and he— in his dark,
salty world, oblivious to the end
waiting for him.

and the clouds were whales

there's something about going home
and the sky moves with you

the clouds, more than vapor
more than they appear to be
and not what they appear most as

it is a fakery—to assume
to set as fact the dissipation of gasses

they stay with me—do these tufts travel
above, beyond, and besides

do you ever walk with clouds
do you ever drink out of the trough of travail
do you ever feel the taste of cherry
                              on your brow
do you quake underneath with sarcophagi

oh manna manna manna
feed my soul with cosmic krill
for i, too, speak the language of whales

this one, with the tail of spades
was with me when i

found you once in bethlehem
eating lemon ice cream like a child searching for taste buds

motion with my lips that
there is a sky yonder to the west of orange and pomegranate

that's where the tooth of blood pierced the rib of adam
the place laid waste to in his absence

for he, keeper of mine, was a landlubber near the seas of sargasso
made mate to mast and folly
who took me to depths where whale jelly lives

down under bilge where barnacle scrapes its existence upon the wood of ages

dry swallow—though i taste the splinter of poplar or pine in the bunker of my aching
returning to the cave of my youth, a misbegotten whale pup, tangled in titans of waves
speak to me the eons of sadness, mother sea
and from your spout issues breath wet with salt
whispering slews of calm for fishermen

this tapestry of clouded whales; you are heavy
yet never the same

you are wet yet you never drown

you are tail and fin and tooth;
yet never fish

you rain upon your enemies of iron ore
yet you are not crucified by the spearman's throw

the oar o' might makes its wave mine
testing all its strength against molecular madness

tell me your troubles master
you reign more than me

Part IV. Reaping

Seasonal

The pines gather densely like old monks,
tall and gaunt
wearing evergreen cloaks

Their brittle fingers pick at each other.
This is the only language they speak.

Other trees gather, willy-nilly,
naked, unlike the brethren
hooded in shadows.

A paved snake winds its way
through the crowd of bark and needle,
tempting winter monasticism to fail.

Air is light and quick
as my vehicle plows its weak resistance.

I want to stop and break a dead branch
—or two
from a poor monk's trunk

But this silly play
hinders not my snake bend,
nor the speed at which I take it.

I plow on.

Wood smoke is pervasive
and copies my paved serpent,
creating barriers among brothers.

Smoke, balsam, and memory
perfume the horizon . . .
whetting my appetite for leisure

and regret.

In pursuit of a holiday,
I have found solitude—

and Satori.

Popular Poplar

In the neighbor's yard it stood, proud and popular.
A poplar of old make that took children into its bone-
colored arms and carried them to heights with lime green hands.

It was here that play accented the tree, giving birth
to new branch recruits, and limbs sprouted more than
enough children to bend a now tired arm toward trunk and root.

Giant arthritic fingers crested the dirt at its base,
giving trips to stumbling youths who would
climb the smooth thick spine.

A ponytail or two might be tugged for balance,
if tight-roping single file, as cracks and shuffles
echoed at summer dusks.

These were days for the preponderant poplar, celebrated
in the annals of a child's forgotten dreams. Scions
of the aged who first saluted the tree when it was still green

on the inside, would hang like bats from stalactites,
their feet pretzeled around knotted boughs,
flapping jellied arms, hissing and screeching.

Today, it stands in autumnal glory, too slick to climb
and too old to carry. The tired tree waits to fall and crumble.

The Descent of the Night Purple

It was coming home that I noticed an October night sky like the skin of a concord grape stretched across the horizon. A vast image, easy to see, as I crested a winding hill-road, with stars like snow crystals fixed against the backdrop of spilt wine. My daughter was listening to Jim Morrison trying to break on through one last time as we descended a straight path that branched down from the hilltop curve. I could still see the faint rind of sunlight meshed behind and through the trees when I felt the transformation, my body shrinking and traveling backwards through the tunnel of time. There, I'm eight or nine, barefoot in my front yard, more excited than I would be in backyard play because there was no fence guarding me from the road and the world beyond. It was open and dark at eight thirty or nine, and I could hear my father on the porch rustling through wicker and umbrellas for his walking stick. He'd appear on the upper step about to descend with a stick splayed across his broad shoulders, palms resting on either end, crucified in anticipation of the coming night walk. He would motion me with a word and a jerk of the head to follow, leaving my mother and sister behind and in the house to turn a TV dial right or left. Then, familiar houses, darkened by shadow, save for dim yellow lamplight in a window or two would be left behind as we bent knee after bent knee up the steep hill. Once there, we'd veer to the left after some twenty paces and meander our way through a mild curve that would fall like bending licorice beneath the oaks and maples. I would look for the mulberries that had already been taken by blue jays and robins two months before, forgetting to watch the path that curved up and right like a rattlesnake tail.

Here, an old poplar tree, a friend of ours, had a long arm, its left I think, that stretched over the road. It was high enough we couldn't touch it and large and long enough to leave its shadow that snaked across the night's pavement. It would then be hurdled by my quick skip and I could hear my father's smooth, even voice tell a story about a great anaconda that awoke at night to stretch its terrible long body along a warm and empty road. But my father and I would never make it home because Jim would finally break through, in the end, and I would pull into my own driveway ready to sing my daughter to sleep. Though, somewhere, in the night purple, a branch long cut down by now, wound its way round two ambling souls who ventured from the threshold of their open door.

The Swarm

A small tornado of wing-ed death peckers

Dear
        invisible
                corpse

where you may lie is beyond my reach,
beyond my sense of smell,
too far from the crowded huddle of corpses

that we will become.

Yours is a place in a field
                or by a wood
                              soft and dark

Somewhere in the shallow grasses of a nigh winter's edge
there,
        by the parched plain,

you're curled into yourself,
the last vestige of a prenatal spawn.

How you died!

before you were born, the warmth
you must have felt—

Your mother ate the clover of life,
chewing the cud of satisfaction;

she gave you a chill when you were birthed
and anointed you with her tongue, as you cried
and snuggled your way to her breast,

but the terrible implementation of time gives way
to a fetal death curl
                        there, where the great   black
      birds

of corruption swarm to a frenzy.

The Last Sky

Stretched before me,
a fractured horizon of
red, orange, and billowy black

as if a volcano cracked the ether
with apocalyptic eruption

My palm cradles my head
and I float on pads of lilies,
peering at the coming extinction
through the fingers of my other hand

I imagine the dinosaurs' last sky
on a cruise through
this python's curve
of a lazy river

To thumb a tooth
from a long extinct lizard
of terrible proportion

. . . to feel the pricking point of its legacy

Blood from my bitten lip
reminds me
that there was none
when monsters turned to ash

Oh mighty asteroid!
hurling gallstone from space . . .

where is your chance encounter
—now?

Do you know where I live?
Do you know that I left
my home
to wander the last days

of my species?

I am here!
Beckoning . . .
waiting for your deliverance
Scores have built temples to you
through their artifice
through their industry

They have summoned you—
made you anew
in their image

Yet I search for the source . . .
the universe's fastball
to strike at the throat
of all those who can't swallow

a tilt in our turn could mean
the end . . .
but, no matter
all is as it will be
I forge a spectacle of bereavement
to caress my darkened cheek
as I give you, my destroyer,
the other to strike!

The Lost Quiet

It isn't so much the noise
as it is the noise that deafens
the silence

The quiet rap of branch on branch,
the crackles of leaf tornadoes in November gales

Where is the acorn hiding,
the one that fell and wasn't heard
for the sound of machine and man

How does the odyssey of otter play out
in quiet water
without a bending ear

In most, a plug of streaming sound
to make pleasant of an afternoon
in gray rooms, peopled with swishing pants

A window might as well be a frame,
admired for its placement

The only honor—
to meet the one who owns the view
without ever having been to its horizon

This sad tale of two dimensions
screeches in time, mesmerizes in place,
leaving us satisfied with our dissatisfaction

We miss the *awahhh* of the fox,
the *yee yee yaaa* of the coyote,
the creature sounds the moon makes

One can stand at the sill and want
to touch the melting orange
upon the slope of the distant grave of day

And cry for our youthful orgy of woebegone
when we laughed and cried with now dead lovers
and comrades

It is a sitting kind of death, behind the glass
in the realm of hum and stroke and
percolating pomposity

We sanitize our brows with jobs well done
and desecrate our souls with the sound of
fluorescence

It is the end of beginning,
the death of sound . . . and sense

Samsara Serenade

a fanning of banana leaves
a scrape of bamboo

the subtle sounds of an eastern
        sunset

an intake of breath
a slow exhale
the yellow of a horizon behind my eyelids

i want an end to it

the suffering of ages
a thought that plagues
my breath count

i must disassemble
to reassemble
to unlearn the ignorance

that has waylaid me

i am indebted to the springs in my pallet
the soft sands of my floor
these things that do not belong

here, in my meditation upon them

1, 2, 3, 4, a sharp
pain in the middle of my foot
a cramp that retracts four of my toes

a nuanced nuisance

that interrupts, bequeathing
another foray into life after birth
i taste the salt of 500-year-old sweat

that imperiously drops down the nose
of my death mask
a legacy of awareness and merit

then and now and later
all, now
faces melt into a full
horizon of unmasking

a breath that has been held

for waves of ages
and the thin edge of paper
bent backward

as a memory

speaks to the assembly of selves
that have gathered
and the naked door opens

About the Author

Khalil Elayan is a Senior Lecturer of English at Kennesaw State University, teaching mostly World and African American Literature. He received his Ph.D. from Georgia State University, focusing on Modern American and Comparative literatures. Along with poetry, his other interests include writing shorts stories, creative nonfiction, and spending time in nature on his farm in north Georgia tending to his blackberries and pepper plants.

Khalil's poems have been published in *Snapdragon: A Journal of Art & Healing, The Black Fork Review, About Place Journal,* and *The Esthetic Apostle*. Khalil's most recent creative nonfiction appears in *Talking Writing* and his short story "No Quedo Mas Nada" was shortlisted for the *Vincent Brothers Review* Annual Short Story Contest and has just been nominated for the Pushcart Prize. Most of his work focuses on the natural environment, climate change, and trauma poetry, giving voice to places and people who may cry out unheard.

www.ingramcontent.com/pod-product-compliance
Lightning Source LLC
Chambersburg PA
CBHW070939160426
43193CB00011B/1741